Jouer Un Rôle

Jouer Un Rôle

Paul Norris

Macmillan Education

First published 1986

Published by
MACMILLAN EDUCATION LTD
Houndmills, Basingstoke, Hampshire RG21 2XS
and London
Companies and representatives
throughout the world

Typeset in Great Britain by
Vine & Gorfin Limited, Exmouth
Printed in Hong Kong

British Library Cataloguing in Publication Data
Norris, Paul
    Jouer un rôle1. French language—Readers
    I. Title
    448.6′421   PC2117

    ISBN 0–333–38838–0

Contents

Preface

This is a book for pupils in their first and second years of French. It contains ten short plays, each subdivided into three self-contained scenes, involving two, three or four characters. These have been given an initial letter, rather than a name, so that pupils can have the fun of making their own choice from the list provided. For the most part the characters can be played by either boys or girls and the necessary allowances are made within the scripts.

In order to make the situation and mood easily understood, there is a synopsis of the action before each scene. This is in English, as are all stage directions, so that pupils' efforts can be concentrated on the spoken French.

At the end of each play there is:

(a) an alternative ending which the pupils can translate

(b) a set of ten questions and answers, combined with a cloze exercise, for oral or written reinforcement

(c) a French language game.

In any one scene a character has no more than eight to ten lines so that the parts can be easily learnt by beginners. The addition of simple props and costumes would give the pupils a chance to put on a 'production' to show the progress they are making in French. Some language departments may have access to video equipment, and the short scenes are ideally suited to video techniques. For the more self-conscious participants, home-made sock puppets may help to overcome camera shyness and encourage a freer use of voice as parts could be read.

Jouer Un Rôle offers opportunities to harness the excitement that many pupils feel at the prospect of learning a foreign language, by offering a sense of enjoyment and enthusiasm and, through that, oral confidence.

1

Le Rendez-vous

(2 characters, 3 scenes)

Two young friends, C_____ and M_____

Choose their names:

Les garçons	*Les filles*
Claude	Chantal
Christophe	Claire
Charles	Colette
Maurice	Marie
Marc	Michelle
Marcel	Maxime

1

In Scene I, C_____ phones M_____ to suggest they go to see a film that evening. M_____ agrees, and they arrange to meet at 7.30, at the corner of the road.

Scene 1

(C_____ picks up the telephone and dials six digits, saying the number aloud in French. Choose your own numbers.)

C: *(Dialling)* X . . X . . X . . X . . X . . X

(The phone rings and M_____ answers it)

M: Allô?

C: Allô, M . . . . .?

M: Oui.

C: Bonjour! C'est moi, C . . . . .

M: Bonjour, C . . . . . . Ça va?

C: Oui, ça va bien. Et toi?

M: Oui, bien.

C: Ecoute. Il y a un film ce soir.

M: Ce soir? Quel film?

C: *L'Homme Invisible.*

M: *L'Homme Invisible*? Formidable!

C: Tu veux venir?

M: *(With enthusiasm)* Bien sûr! Et le rendez-vous?. . . . .

C: Au coin de la rue.

M: A quelle heure?

C: Sept heures et demie?

M: D'accord!

C: A bientôt!

In Scene 2, the friends arrive separately at the rendez-vous and are out of each other's sight on different sides of the corner.
   At 7.30 they each decide to go on alone, and as they walk away they bump into each other.

Scene 2

(C_ _ _ _ _ arrives at the corner, looks around, but canot see M_ _ _ _ _)

C: *(Slightly doubtful)* C'est ici, le rendez-vous?

(M_ _ _ _ _ arrives on the other side of the corner)

M: *(Looks anxiously around)* C'est ici, le rendez-vous?

C: *(Worried)* M_ _ _ _ _ n'est pas ici.

M: *(Paces up and down)* C_ _ _ _ _ n'est pas ici.

C: Quelle heure est-il? *(Looks at wrist-watch)*

M: *(Looks up at church clock)* Il est sept heures et demie.

C: Sept heures et demie!

M: C_ _ _ _ _ est en retard.

C: *(Impatiently)* Le film commence à huit heures.

M: *(Annoyed)* Oh! Quelle barbe!

C: C'est un film fantastique.

M: C'est un film magnifique.

C: *(Angrily)* Zut! M_____ ne vient pas.

M: *(Disappointed)* Eh bien, je m'en vais! . . .

(At this point they both decide not to wait any longer and move off, bumping into each other as they reach the corner)

C: *(Surprised)* Oh! C'est toi!

M: *(Relieved)* Oui, c'est moi! Bonjour, C_____!

C: Ecoute, M_____. Nous sommes en retard.

M: Allons vite!

(They hurry off to the cinema)

In Scene 3, the friends, on arriving at the cinema, have a nasty shock when C_____ thinks a twenty-franc note is missing. It is soon found and they go to buy their tickets for the film. At this moment C_____ sees that The Invisible Man *is not on till the following week. Tonight's programme is* Snow White and the Seven Dwarfs.

Scene 3

(C_____ and M_____ arrive outside the cinema. They have been hurrying and are out of breath)

C: *(Panting)* Voilà le cinéma!

M: *(Gasping)* Oui, le voilà!

C: *(Searching through pockets)* Attends!

M: *(Impatiently)* Pourquoi? Qu'as-tu encore?

C: Mon billet de vingt francs! . . .

M: *(Puzzled)* Quoi? Ton billet de vingt francs?

C: *(Desperately)* Je ne le trouve pas.

M: C'est impossible!

C: Il n'est pas dans ma poche.

M: Tu es sûr?

C: Oui, certain *(Suddenly finds the money)* . . . Non! Le voici!

M: Ouf! Allons vite! Il est presque huit heures.

C: *(With horror)* Oh, non! Regarde!

M: *(Losing patience)* Quoi, encore!

C: *(Pointing to the poster outside the cinema)* L'Homme Invisible . . .

M: Et alors?

C: C'est la semaine prochaine.

M: *(Furious)* Oh, bon sang! Et ce soir?

C: *(Laughing)* Blanche-Neige . . .

M: *(Joining in the joke)* Et les Sept Nains!

(They walk off laughing together)

Try giving the last scene a different ending. Start from the line of dots after M_____ says: 'Quoi encore!' Read the dialogue below and see if you can understand what happens.

M: Quoi encore!

C: Oh, non! Tu as tes vingt francs?

M: Oui. Bien sûr!

C: Ce n'est pas assez.

M: *(Incredulous)* Sans blague!

C: Regarde le tarif. Vingt-cinq francs!

M: Nom d'un chien! J'ai seulement vingt francs.

C: Moi, j'ai trente francs.

M: Eh bien, C_____, mon ami.

C: Oui?

M: Prête-moi cinq francs, s'il te plaît.

C: Je suis trop généreux/généreuse!

M: Allons! Le film commence.

Et maintenant

Le Quiz

Tu es M_ _ _ _ _

1 Vas-tu au cinéma?
   Oui, je _____ au_____.

2 Comment s'appelle ton ami(e)?
   Mon ami(e) s'appelle _____.

3 Où rencontres-tu ton ami(e)?
   Je rencontre mon _____ au _____ de la
   _____.

4 A quelle heure rencontres-tu ton ami(e)?
   Je rencontre _____ ami(e) à _____ heures et
   _____.

5 Quel film vas-tu voir?
   Je _____ voir L'_____ _____.

6 Vois-tu ton ami(e) au coin de la rue?
   Non, je ne _____ pas mon _____.

7 Est-il (elle) en retard?
   Oui, il (elle) _____ en _____.

8 A quelle heure commence le film?
   Le film _____ à _____ heures.

9 Où est le billet de vingt francs?
   Le billet _____ dans _____ poche.

10 Quel film passe-t-il au cinéma?
   C'est *Blanche* _____ *et les* _____ *Nains.*

Et ensuite . . .

Le Jeu

Alibis

Two of you join with another pair to make a group
of four. Two of you are French detectives who do
not speak English.

A crime has been committed, and the other two
have to provide an alibi for that particular evening
when they went to the cinema together. (All the
facts are as in the play.)

To make it more realistic, the detectives can read
their questions from 'Le Quiz'.

The 'suspects', who should be interrogated
separately, will not have anything to refer to. They
have to remember what happened. Their answers
will be noted down.

Do their stories agree? If so, they will be
released. If not, they may be detained for further
questioning . . . !

2

Une Question de Reconnaissance

(3 characters, 3 scenes)

Two friends, P_____ and J_____
P_____'s English penfriend, K_____

Choose their names:

Les garçons	Les filles
Pascal	Pierrette
Pierre	Pauline
Patrice	Priscilla
Jérome	Jeanne
Jules	Josephine
Justin	Juliette
Keith	Kathleen
Kenneth	Kim
Kevin	Karen

*P_____ and J_____ have come to the main Gare du Nord
station in Paris to meet K_____, P_____'s English
penfriend, who is arriving on the train from Calais.*

Scene 1

*(P_____ and J_____ come out of the Métro into the noise
and bustle of the main terminus of the Gare du Nord)*

P: Ah! nous voici!

J: Mais quel train?

P: Attends. *(Takes a letter out and looks at it)*

J: *(Puts hands over ears)* Zut! Quel bruit!

P: *(Loudly)* Le train de Calais.

J: C'est tout?

P: *(Studying letter carefully)* K_____ arrive à midi.

J: Mais sur quelle voie?

P: Je ne sais pas.

*(The voice of the Station Announcer comes over the
loudspeaker. The person playing K_____ can take this part.)*

ANNOUNCER: Allô, allô . . .

J: Ecoute!

P: Quoi?

J: Chut! . . . *(Points to Train Arrival board)*

ANNOUNCER: Le train de Calais arrive sur la voie dix à midi.

P: Voie dix. C'est là-bas!

J: Quelle heure est-il?

P: *(Looks up at station clock)* Presque midi.

J: Vite! Le train arrive!

(They hurry towards the barrier of Platform 10)

*P_____ and J_____ are at the barrier of Platform 10,
Looking out for K_____. They do not have a photo but
P_____ thinks that it will be easy to spot someone speaking
English. Unfortunately, several school parties from England get
off the train!*

Scene 2

*(P_____ and J_____ are standing at the barrier of Platform
10, watching the train come into the station)*

P: Nous cherchons un jeune Anglais/une jeune Anglaise.

J: *(Puzzled)* C'est tout?

P: *(Confidently)* Oui.

J: Tu n'as pas de photo?

P: Non.

J: Tu peux reconnaître K_____?

P: Oui. C'est un Anglais/une Anglaise!

J: *(Unconvinced)* Oh, oui . . . ça suffit?

P: *(Explaining carefully)* K_____ va parler anglais.

J: Ah! Pas de problème, alors!

*(The train comes to a halt. Doors open and passengers come
pouring through the barrier. There are several parties of
English schoolchildren.)*

P: *(With horror)* Mais non! Regarde!

J: Oh, bon sang!

P: Toute la population de l'Angleterre est là!

J: *(Anxiously)* Tu vois K_____?

P: *(Worried)* Non.

(At this moment K_____ walks past them, waits looking around and then moves away towards the telephones)

In Scene 3, P_____ decides to phone home to say that K_____ has not arrived. However, the phone-boxes are all occupied and they wait outside one of them. It is, by chance, the one that K_____ is using to telephone P_____'s mother. They overhear the conversation and introduce themselves to K_____.

Scene 3

(K_____ enters a telephone box, and takes out a piece of paper and a coin. Studies instructions on how to use the telephone. P_____ and J_____ stand talking some way away)

P: Je vais téléphoner à ma mère.

J: Où est la cabine?

P: Là-bas.

J: Tu as de l'argent?

P: Oui, j'ai un franc.

(They hurry towards the telephone box. K_____ has just started speaking to P_____'s mother.)

K: *(Speaking into telephone)* Allô, Madame Dupont?

P: La cabine est occupée.

K: *(Into phone)* C'est K_____.

J: *(Hears what K_____ has said)* Ecoute!

K: *(Into phone)* Je suis à la gare, Madame Dupont.

P: *(Listening)* C'est K_____?

J: Bien sûr!

K: *(Into phone)* Je ne vois pas P_____.

P: *(Excitedly)* Oui, c'est K_____. *(Taps on window of telephone box)*

K: *(Into phone)* Un moment, Madame. *(Opens door of box)*

P: Excusez moi. Je suis P_____ Dupont. Vous êtes K_____?

K: *(Into phone)* P_____ est ici, Madame. Au revoir. A tout à l'heure.

(K_____ comes out of phone box and is greeted by P_____ and J_____)

P: *(With great relief)* Salut, K_____!

J: *(Enthusiastically)* Salut, K_____!

K: Thank heavens you're here!

P and J: *(Together)* En français, K_____, en français!

(They exit chatting together in French)

P_____ was lucky to find K_____ in the busy Gare du Nord. In an alternative last scene below, P_____ has a good idea and does manage to meet K_____ on Platform 10. Read the dialogue to find out what happens.

P: Vite! Un crayon!

J: Pourquoi?

P: Je vais écrire son nom sur du papier. *(He takes a piece of paper from his pocket)*

J: Et tu vas montrer le papier?

P: K_ _ _ _ _ va lire le papier et . . .

J: Et voilà! Quelle bonne idée!

K: Excusez-moi? *(When he sees his name on the paper)*

P: Oui?

K: Vous êtes P_ _ _ _ _?

P: Oui.

K: Vous cherchez K_ _ _ _ _?

P: Oui.

K: Eh bien, c'est moi! Bonjour P_ _ _ _ _ _.

P: Mais vous parlez français!

K: Naturellement!

P: Pourquoi 'naturellement'?

K: En Angleterre, j'apprends le français à l'école!

(Can you think of the other ways P_ _ _ _ _ could have found K_ _ _ _ _?)

Et maintenant

Le Quiz

Tu es P_ _ _ _ _

1 Attends-tu le train de Calais?
   Oui, j'attends le _____ de _____.

2 A quelle heure arrive le train?
   Le train _____ à _____.

3 Sur quelle voie arrive le train?
   Le train arrive _____ voie _____.

4 As-tu la photo de K_ _ _ _ _?
   Non, je n' _____ pas _____ photo de
   K_ _ _ _ _.

5 Peux-tu reconnaître K_ _ _ _ _?
   Oui, je _____ reconnaître K_ _ _ _ _.

6 Va-t-il (elle) parler anglais?
   Oui, il (elle) _____ parler _____.

7 Vas-tu téléphoner à ta mère?
   Oui, je _____ téléphoner à _____ mère.

8 As-tu de l'argent?
   Oui, j'ai un _____.

9 Qui est dans la cabine?
   _____ _____ dans _____ cabine.

10 A qui téléphone-t-il (elle)?
   Il (Elle) _____ à _____ mère.

Et ensuite . . .

Le Jeu

The Oui/Non Game

Work with a partner or a small group.

One person asks the questions, using those in 'Le Quiz'. The person who is answering must reply in French, without using the words *oui* or *non*.

If either *oui* or *non* are said, or the person nods or shakes his head, the *questioner* scores a point.

Everyone should have a turn as questioner.

Now invent your own questions, in French, to try to trap the others. Here are five to start you off:

'Parles-tu anglais?'

'As-tu les yeux bleus?'

'Habites-tu à Paris?'

'Es-tu dans la salle de classe?'

'As-tu douze ans?'

You can make a list of your questions to help you to remember them.

3

Chez Pagaille

(4 characters, 3 scenes)

Two waiters/waitresses   D_ _ _ _ _ and G_ _ _ _ _
Two customers   B_ _ _ _ _ and R_ _ _ _ _

Choose their names:

Waiters/waitresses	*Customers*
Les garçons	*Les garçons*
Didier	Bernard
Dominique	Bertrand
Daniel	Bruno
Gaston	Rémi
Gérard	Renaud
Gustave	Roland
Les filles	*Les filles*
Delphine	Blanche
Diana	Brigitte
Denise	Bettina
Gisèle	Rosalie
Grâce	Renée
Ginette	Roseline

CHEZ PAGAILLE

MENU à 50 francs

Potage du jour
ou
Moules à la crème

Blanquette de veau
ou
Coq au vin

Fromage ou salade

Dessert

(Taxe et service compris)

The scene takes place in the restaurant Chez Pagaille. *The restaurant is empty when R_____ enters and is served by G_____. R_____ orders an apéritif and is given the menu. B_____ enters, sits at a different table, studies the menu but refuses a drink. G_____ exits behind the bar. D_____ brings in the apéritif and gives it to B_____ by mistake.*

Scene 1

(The restaurant is empty. R_____ enters and is welcomed by G_____.)

G: Bonsoir, monsieur/madame.

R: Bonsoir.

G: Vouse désirez déjeuner, monsieur/madame?

R: Oui, merci.

G: Ici, s'il vous plaît. *(Sits R_____ down at table)*

R: Merci.

G: Un apéritif, Monsieur/madame?

R: Oui! un Pernod, s'il vous plaît.

G: Merci, monsieur. La carte.

   (G_____ gives R_____ the menu and hands the drink order to D_____ B_____ enters and is welcomed by G_____.)

G: Bonsoir, monsicur/madame.

B: Bonsoir. Puis-je déjeuner, s'il vous plaît?

G: Certainement, monsieur/madame. *(Shows B_____ to seat)*

B: Merci.

G: Un apéritif, monsieur/madame?

B: Non, merci.

G: La carte, monsieur/madame. *(Hands B_____ menu)*

B: Merci.

   (G_____ goes out and D_____ comes in and goes over to B_____'s table)

D: Votre Pernod, monsieur/madame.

B: Je ne veux pas de Pernod.

D: Comment?

R: Le Pernod est pour moi.

D: Ah, c'est pour vous, monsieur/madame.

R: Oui.

D: *(To B_____)* Je m'excuse, monsieur/madame.

B: Cela ne fait rien.

   In Scene 2 D_____ takes the orders from R_____ and B_____.

Scene 2

D: *(To R_____)* Monsieur/madame a choisi?

R: Oui. *(Reads from menu)* Potage du jour et blanquette de veau.

D: *(Repeats order)* Potage du jour et blanquette de veau.

R: Oui.

D: Et comme boisson?

R: Une carafe de vin rouge.

D: Une carafe. Merci, monsieur/madame. *(Goes over to B_____)* Monsieur/madame a choisi?

B: Oui, moules à la crème et coq au vin.

D: Moules à la crème et coq au vin.

B: Oui.

D: Et comme boisson?

B: Une bière.

D: Merci, monsieur/madame. *(Exits with orders)*

In Scene 3, there are more muddles when the food is served. Even with only two customers, G_____ mixes up the two orders. The food is so good, however, that the customers don't mind the muddle.

Scene 3

(G_____ enters carrying a tray)

G: *(To R_____)* Les moules à la crème pour monsieur/madame.

R: Je ne veux pas de moules.

G: Mais, monsieur/madame! . . .

R: Je veux du potage.

B: Les moules sont pour moi.

G: Oh, je m'excuse! Bon appétit, monsieur/madame. *(Goes out and brings in soup)* Votre potage, monsieur/madame.

R: Merci.

G: Bon appétit. *(Goes out and brings in the carafe of wine which he offers to B_ _ _ _ _)* Votre vin rouge, monsieur/madame.

B: Je ne veux pas de vin.

G: Oh, pardon! monsieur/madame.

R: Le vin est pour moi.

G: Ah, bon! Voilà, monsieur/madame.

R: Merci.

(G_ _ _ _ _ goes out)

R: C'est toujours la même chose ici.

B: Mais quelle cuisine!

R: Oui, c'est délicieux!

(They tuck into their food)

The play Chez Pagaille *has a happy ending after all the problems are sorted out. Read the alternative ending below and see what* could *have happened!*

G: *(To R_ _ _ _ _)* Moules à la crème, monsieur/madame.

R: Je ne veux pas de moules.

G: Mais, monsieur/madame! . . .

B: Les moules sont pour moi.

G: Ah bon . . . *(Drops the plate into B_ _ _ _ _'s lap)*

B: Aïeeee! Quel imbécile!

G: Je suis désolé . . . *(Tries to clean B_ _ _ _ _)*

B: Laissez-moi tranquille!

G: Vite, D . . . . ., de l'eau!

(D_____ rushes in, slips on the mussels and throws the water on to R_____)

R: Aïeeee! Arrghh! Faites attention!

D: Oh, pardon, monsieur/madame . . .

R: Ça suffit. Je m'en vais!

B: Et moi, aussi.

(They storm out. D_____ shuts the door and puts up the 'FERMÉ' sign.)

G: Tu as faim, D . . . . .?

D: Bien sûr.

G: Eh bien, viens manger!

D: Bon appétit!

Et maintenant

Le Quiz

Tu ès R_ _ _ _ _

1 Veux-tu déjeuner?
   Oui, je _____ déjeuner.

2 Quel apéritif veux-tu?
   Je veux un _____.

3 As-tu la carte?
   Oui, j'_____ la carte.

4 As-tu choisi?
   Oui, j'ai _____.

5 Veux-tu du potage?
   Oui, je _____ du _____.

6 Veux-tu du vin rouge?
   Oui, je _____ du _____ rouge.

7 Aimes-tu les moules?
   Non, je n'_____ pas _____ moules.

8 Veux-tu du coq au vin?
   _____, je ne veux _____ de coq _____ vin.

9 Aimes-tu le restaurant?
   _____. j'_____ bien le _____.

10 La cuisine, est-elle bonne?
    Oui, la _____ est _____.

Et ensuite...

Le Jeu

The Right Order

For 2 to 10 people.

The first person says:

'Je vais au restaurant pour manger _____', giving any item of food from the list on the next page.

The next person says:

'Je vais au restaurant pour manger _____', (the food the first person chose) 'et _____', (an item of their own choice.)

and so on...

Example:

A. Je vais au restaurant pour manger du jambon.
B. Je vais au restaurant pour manger du jambon et des escargots.
C. Je vais au restaurant pour manger du jambon, des escargots et du porc.

Remember: the items of food must be named in *the right order*, and no item can be used twice in the same game.

When the chain of orders is broken, start a new one! On page 26 is a list of foods to choose from.

FOOD FOR THE GAME!

du potage – soup
des moules – mussels
des escargots – snails
du homard – lobster
une assiette anglaise – cold meat
du poisson – fish
du boeuf – beef
du poulet – chicken
du veau – veal
un bifteck – steak
des crevettes roses – prawns
des carottes – carrots
du jambon – ham
des haricots verts – green beans
des pommes frites – chips
une omelette – omelette
du fromage – cheese
de la salade – salad
un dessert – dessert
une tarte aux pommes – apple flan
un sorbet – sorbet ice-cream
une glace – ice-cream

4

En Route

(3 main characters, 2 minor characters; 3 scenes)

The main characters:

Monsieur Leclerc (P)   Madame Leclerc (M)
Their child   V_ _ _ _ _

Choose the child's name:

Les garçons	*Les filles*
Victor	Valérie
Vincent	Véronique
Valentin	Vivienne

The minor characters:

A farmer (F)   A garage mechanic (Gar)
In the alternative ending there is a gendarme (G).

The Leclerc family are going on holiday. In Scene 1, Monsieur Leclerc is putting the luggage in the car and is anxious to get started. At last everyone is ready and they drive off. Suddenly Madame Leclerc realises she has forgotten her handbag and has to get it. Then V_____ goes back to get a ball. Finally, they begin the journey.

Scene 1

(All three are helping to put things in the car. Papa is getting impatient. Maman and V_____ keep going back into the house.)

P: *(Calling out)* Quelle heure est-il?

M: *(Calls back)* Il est dix heures.

V: *(Excitedly)* Oh! il est dix heures!

P: *(Impatiently)* Vite! Nous sommes en retard.

(Maman and V_____ get in the car. They drive off.)

V: *(Calls out)* Au revoir maison! Au revoir jardin!

M: Oh non, mon sac à main! Où est-il?

P: Mais non! *(Papa reverses car back to house)* Les dames!

M: *(Getting out of car)* Merci, chéri. *(Maman dashes into house and comes back with her handbag)*

P: C'est tout?

V: Oh non, mon ballon! *(V_____ gets out and comes back with his/her ball)*

P: Les enfants!

V: Le voilà! Merci, Papa.

P: Enfin! Sommes-nous prêts?

M: Oui, chéri.

P: Vous êtes sûr(e)s?

V and M: Oui, Papa.

(They drive away quickly)

In Scene 2, the family are playing a car game as they drive along. Maman is enjoying the game and forgets to look at the map. They get lost, but, thanks to directions from a helpful farmer, are soon on their way again.

Scene 2

(The family are playing a car game of spotting particular items, and scoring points. They are having fun.)

V: Regarde! Une chèvre!

P: Un point.

M: *(Pointing)* Et là-bas . . . un canard.

P: Trois points.

V: *(Getting very excited)* Un cheval brun! Regarde.

P: Deux points.

V: *(Very excitedly)* Et une tulipe!

P: Cinq points.

M: *(Victoriously)* Regarde! Un taureau!

P: Sept points. Tu gagnes, chérie.

V: Encore! Un autre jeu!

M: Un moment ... où sommes-nous? *(Maman looks about her and peers hopefully at the map)*

P: Comment? Tu ne sais pas?

M: Non, chéri.

V: *(Tearfully)* Nous sommes perdus!

M: *(Positively)* Nous allons demander le chemin à un fermier.

(They see a farmer and stop to ask him the way)

P: La route pour aller à Deauville, s'il vous plaît?

F: *(Scratching his head)* La route pour Deauville?

P: Oui.

F: Ah, oui! Deauville ... c'est là-bas! *(He points back the way they have just come)*

M: Oh, non!

F: Prenez la première rue à droite ...:

M: Oui.

F: Et continuez tout droit.

M: Merci mille fois.

V: Au revoir.

(Papa drives off even faster than before)

Scene 3 finds the family driving happily along when, suddenly, the engine splutters and the car stops. Papa is annoyed when Maman asks if they have run out of petrol. V_____ spots a garage and they push the car into the forecourt. The garagiste confirms that they have run out of petrol. He fills the tank for them but when Papa goes to pay the bill he finds that he has left his wallet at home. Maman is very amused. She pays!

Scene 3

(The family are singing happily as they drive along. Suddenly the car splutters to a halt.)

P: Mais non! C'est impossible!

M: Pourquoi nous arrêtons-nous, chéri?

P: *(Annoyed)* Je ne sais pas, chérie.

M: *(Innocently)* Avons-nous de l'essence?

P: *(Sharply)* Mais oui. Naturellement!

(Papa gets out, opens the bonnet and carefully studies the engine. He cannot see anything wrong.)

V: *(Pointing into the distance)* Papa, regarde, un garage!

P: Bon. Poussons la voiture.

(They push the car, with Maman steering, on to the garage forecourt)

Gar: Bonjour, monsieur. Un problème?

V: Oui, notre voiture est . . .

P: *(Interrupting sharply)* . . . est en panne!

(The garage mechanic has a good look at the car)

Gar: Vous n'avez pas d'essence, monsieur.

P: *(Embarrassed)* Oh! . . . Faites-le plein, s'il vous plaît.

(The mechanic fills the car with petrol)

Gar: Cent vingt francs, monsieur.

P: *(Discovers he has left his wallet at home)* Oh non! Chérie, tu as de l'argent?

M: *(Pleased with herself)* Oh! Tu n'as pas ton portefeuille?

P: Eh bien! . . .

M: Voilà, chérie.

(Maman pays for the petrol and they set off for Deauville)

A motorist can have many problems. Running out of petrol is just one of them. In this alternative ending to the play, the family get into trouble of a different kind.

V: *(Urgently)* Papa, nous allons trop vite!

P: Tais-toi, V_ _ _ _ _!

V: Il y a un gendarme derrière nous.

P: Tais-toi!

(The gendarme overtakes them with his siren wailing and flags them down)

G: Bonjour, monsieur.

P: *(Nervously)* Bonjour.

G: Vous êtes pressé?

M: Oui, nous allons à Deauville.

V: Et nous sommes en retard.

G: Vous roulez trop vite, monsieur.

P: C'est vrai?

G: Votre permis de conduire, monsieur.

P: Ah oui! il est ici. *(He searches frantically in his pockets)*

M: Où est-il, chéri?

V: Il est dans la cuisine, Papa.

P: Oh!

G: Eh bien, roulez moins vite!

P: Certainement, monsieur. Merci.

G: *(Getting back on his bike)* Bon voyage.

M and V: Merci.

(They set off for Deauville at a moderate pace!)

Et maintenant

Le Quiz

Tu es Madame Leclerc.

1 Quelle heure est-il?
   Il est _____ heures.

2 Es-tu en retard?
   Oui, je _____ en retard.

3 Oublies-tu ton sac à main?
   Oui, j'_____ mon _____ à main.

4 Qui oublie son ballon?
   C'est _____ qui oublie _____ ballon.

5 Vois-tu une chèvre?
   Non, je _____ un canard.

6 Gagnes-tu le jeu?
   Oui, je _____ le _____.

7 A qui demandes-tu le chemin?
   Je _____ le _____ à un _____.

8 Prends-tu la rue à gauche ou à droite?
   Je prends _____ rue à _____.

9 Vois-tu un garage?
   Oui, je _____ un garage.

10 As-tu de l'argent?
   Oui, j'_____ beaucoup d'_____.

Et ensuite ...

Le Jeu

The Letter Chain

On a long journey, it helps to pass the time if you play a game. The Leclercs like the one in which points are gained for spotting certain things.

Another is 'The Letter Chain'. You can play it in class, in either pairs or small groups.

The first person says a French word and 'passes' the *last* letter of that word on to the second person.

The second person must say a word that *begins* with this letter, and then pass the last letter of the new word on to the next person, and so on ...

Example:
First person: 'Heure ... E.'
Second person: 'E ... Escargots ... S.'
Third person: 'S ... Sur ... R.'
Fourth person: 'R ... Retard ... D.' etc.
(You can get words from *Jouer Un Rôle* if you get stuck!)

The same words must not be used twice. Anyone who cannot find a new word with the right letter, breaks the chain and loses a point. The person who has lost the fewest points is the winner.

5

C'est du Vol!

(3 characters, 3 scenes)

Two people in the lift   A_____ and B_____

Choose their names:

Les garçons	*Les filles*
André	Annette
Alain	Anne-marie
Alphonse	Adèle
Bernard	Blanche
Bertrand	Béatrice
Blaise	Brigitte

A stranger   X_____

In Scene 1, A_____ and B_____ are waiting for the lift on the ground floor. A_____ suddenly realises that he/she is late for an appointment.

Scene 1

(A_____ and B_____ meet at the ground-floor lift)

A: Bonjour, B_____.

B: Bonjour, A_____. Ça va?

A: Oui, et vous . . . ?

B: Ça va bien, merci.

A: Quelle heure est-il?

B: Huit heures et demie.

A: Oh, non!

B: Vous êtes en retard?

A: Oui, j'ai un rendez-vous.

B: A quelle heure?

A: A huit heures vingt!

B: Vous êtes en retard!

(A_____ paces up and down and presses the lift button several times)

In Scene 2, the lift arrives and just as the doors are about to close, they are joined by a stranger, X. Little knowing that he is a thief, they warn him of the dangers of getting his pockets picked!

Scene 2

(The lift arrives and A_____ and B_____ get in. Just as the doors are closing, a stranger pushes into the lift.)

A: Bonjour!

X: Bonjour!

A: *(Ready to press the lift buttons)* Quel étage?

X: Dix-huitième, s'il vous plaît.

B: Il faut faire attention.

X: A quoi, monsieur/madame?

A: Aux voleurs à la tire! . . .

X: Vraiment?

B: Oui. Dans l'ascenseur.

X: C'est impossible!

A: *(Firmly)* Non, c'est possible!

B: Oui, c'est possible!

X: Mais il est si petit. *(X pushes up against A_____, neatly removing the watch from A_____'s wrist, and slipping it into his pocket)*

A: Comment?

X: *(Pressing up against B_____ and removing a wallet from B_____'s pocket)* Il n'y a pas de place.

A: Oui, c'est vrai.

B: *(Confidently)* Il est trop petit.

(The lift stops)

X: Je sors ici.

A and B: *(Together)* Au revoir.

X: *(Getting out of lift)* Au revoir et merci.

(The lift doors close)

In Scene 3, A_____ and B_____ reach the twentieth floor and get out of the lift. But what's the time? How late is it? Horror of horrors! A_____'s watch has gone and so has B_____'s wallet. The pickpocket has struck again.

Scene 3

(The lift continues its journey)

A: Vous connaissez cet homme?

B: Non, et vous?

A: Non, je ne le connais pas.

B: Il est très aimable.

A: Oui, très gentil. Enfin, le vingtième étage.

(They get out of the lift)

B: Quelle heure est-il?

A: *(Goes to look at his watch)* Il est . . . Où est ma montre?

B: Comment?

A: Je n'ai plus ma montre!

(B_____ checks pocket for wallet)

B: Mon portefeuille! . . .

A: Comment?

B: Je n'ai plus mon portefeuille!

A: Cet homme . . .

B: Le voleur à la tire . . .

A: Ce n'est pas possible!

B: Vite! La police!

(They jump back into the lift and the doors close)

The alternative ending gives a change of villain, so A_____ takes X's watch and B_____ takes X's wallet! Remember that pickpockets often do work in teams! We take up the scene at the point where A_____ and B_____ are discussing X after he got out of the lift.

A: Oui, très gentil.

B: Moi, j'ai sa montre.

A: Elle est très belle!

B: Oui.

A: *(Triumphantly)* Moi, j'ai son portefeuille.

B: Oh, il est très beau!

A: Et plein d'argent!

B: *(Laughing)* Magnifique!

A: Il est très généreux, ce monsieur.

(He presses the ground-floor button)

Et maintenant

Le Quiz

Tu es B_ _ _ _ _.

1   Comment ça va?
    Ça va _____ merci.

2   Quelle heure est-il?
    Il est huit heures et _____.

3   Es-tu en retard?
    Non, je ne _____ pas en retard.

4   A quelle heure est le rendez-vous de A_ _ _ _ _?
    Son rendez-vous est _____ huit heures _____.

5   Faut-il faire attention?
    Oui, il _____ faire attention.

6   L'ascenseur, est-il grand?
    Non, il est _____.

7   Où sors-tu?
    Je sors _____ _____ étage.

8   As-tu ton portefeuille?
    Non, je n'ai pas _____ portefeuille.

9   A_ _ _ _ _, a-t-il/elle sa montre?
    Non, A_ _ _ _ _ n'a pas _____ montre.

10 Es-tu un voleur à la tire?
    Non, je ne _____ pas un voleur à la tire.

Et ensuite...

Le Jeu

Whose Is It?

Each member of the class puts a small object into a box or bag brought round by the teacher. The teacher then takes out one of the objects and asks one of the class:

'A qui est cet objet?'

(The answer can only be a guess, because no one should have seen what each person put in!)

The pupil guesses who put the object in the bag:

'C'est l'objet de _ _ _ _ _.'

If the guess is right, the person who has been named says:

'Oui, c'est mon objet.'

If the guess is wrong, the person who has been named says:

'Non, ce n'est pas mon objet.'

The teacher then asks:

'A qui est cet objet?'

The rightful owner says:

'C'est mon objet.'

Scoring: TWO points for correctly guessing the owner. ONE point for each other correct response.

NB The word 'objet' can be changed for the specific name of the item, e.g. 'A qui est cette gomme?' 'C'est la gomme de _ _ _ _ _.' 'Oui, c'est ma gomme.'

6

Le Raccourci

(2 characters, 3 scenes)

The driver of the car:

Le Chauffeur   C_ _ _ _ _

The pedestrian:

Le Piéton   P_ _ _ _ _

43

In Scene 1, the driver of the car is in a strange town and is looking for The Bank of France. A pedestrian is asked for directions and agrees to go in the car as the route is rather complicated.

Scene 1

(The driver pulls the car over to the side of the road and winds down the window)

C: Pardon, monsieur/madame . . .

P: Oui, monsieur/madame.

C: Connaissez-vous cette ville?. . . . .

P: Parfaitement, monsieur/madame.

C: Eh bien, je cherche la Banque de France.

P: Je la connais bien, monsieur/madame.

C: Formidable!

P: Mais elle est loin d'ici.

C: C'est dommage!

P: Et la route est très difficile.

C: Oh, non! Et moi, je suis en retard!

P: Rassurez-vous! J'habite près de la banque et je connais le chemin.

C: Magnifique! Montez dans la voiture.

P: Merci, monsieur/madame.

(P_ _ _ _ _ gets into the car and they drive off)

In Scene 2, they set off through the town and the driver finds the pedestrian's directions more and more complicated.

Scene 2

P: Prenez la première rue à droite.

C: Ici?

P: Oui. Et la deuxième rue à gauche.

C: *(Peering anxiously out of the car window)* Première ... deuxième ... Rue Blague?

P: C'est ça. Allez tout droit.

C: Il fait beau, n'est-ce pas?

P: Oui. *(Suddenly shouting)* Attention! Les feux sont rouges!

C: *(Brakes hastily)* Oh! Merci! La route est très compliquée.

P: Oui. A gauche ici.

C: Avenue de la Ruse?

P: Oui. Allez tout droit maintenant.

(They drive on. C_ _ _ _ _ has absolutely no idea where they are.)

In Scene 3, the driver is puzzled to see that they are leaving the town. When, finally, they stop the bank is nowhere to be seen. The pedestrian has just saved the bus fare home!

Scene 3

C: *(Worried)* Mais nous quittons la ville! ...

P: *(Soothingly)* Oui, mais c'est un raccourci.

C: Oh, je comprends.

P: Arrêtez-vous ici.

C: *(Looking round for the bank)* A gauche ou à droite?

P: A droite.

(The car stops and the pedestrian gets out)

C: Pardon, monsieur/madame.

P: *(Moving back to the car)* Oui?

C: Où est la banque?

P: La banque?

C: Oui, j'ai un rendez-vous . . .

P: *(Blankly)* Je ne sais pas, monsieur/madame.

C: La barbe!

P: *(Apologetically)* Les autobus sont très chers.

C: *(Furious)* Zut alors!

P: Merci mille fois! *(Walks cheerfully away)*

C: *(Almost speechless with annoyance)* Sacrebleu! *(Drives off at speed)*

Now try this ending. . . . The driver is not quite the innocent, lost tourist as might first have appeared. Can you see why he/she really wanted to get to the bank?

(The car pulls up outside the bank)

C: Ah, voilà la banque!

P: Oui, la Banque de France.

C: Merci mille fois!

P: Je vous en prie.

C: Au revoir! *(C_____ and P_____ get out of the car)*

P: Vous n'arrêtez pas le moteur?

C: Non. Je suis pressé.

P: Au revoir!

   (C_____ runs into the bank)

C: *(To someone in the bank, menacingly)* Mettez tout l'argent dans ce sac. Vite, ou je tire!

   (Carrying a bag full of money, C_____ runs out of the bank and gets in the car quickly)

C: Au revoir!

P: *(Turning round)* Bon sang! C'est un gangster!

C: Et merci, eh!

   (C_____ drives away)

Et maintenant

Le Quiz

Tu es le chauffeur C_ _ _ _ _.

1 Que cherches-tu?
   Je cherche la _____.

2 Es-tu à l'heure?
   Non, je suis en _____.

3 Comment est la route?
   La route est très _____.

4 Qui monte dans ta voiture?
   Le piéton monte dans _____ voiture.

5 Quelle rue prends-tu à droite?
   Je prends la _____ rue à droite.

6 Quel temps fait-il?
   Il fait _____.

7 La route, est-elle simple?
   Non, elle est très _____.

8 Quittez-vous la ville?
   Oui, nous _____ la ville.

9 Où t'arrêtes-tu, à gauche ou à droite?
   Je m'arrête à _____.

10 Vois-tu la banque?
    Non, je ne la _____ pas.

Et ensuite . . .

Le Jeu

The game is played in the same way as the English game 'Simon says . . .'

If an instruction begins with . . . 'Jacques a dit . . .' then it must be obeyed. YOU ARE *OUT* IF YOU DON'T DO THE CORRECT ACTION *IMMEDIATELY*.

If an instruction is given *without* using 'Jacques a dit' no action must be taken. YOU ARE OUT IF YOU OBEY IT.

> E.g. 'Levez la main gauche!'
> (You must *not* raise your left hand.)
>
> 'Jacques a dit: levez la main gauche!'
> (You *must* raise your left hand.)

The winner is the one who is left when everyone else is OUT.

Here are some instructions that may be useful:

> Levez le pied gauche/droit.
> Baissez le pied gauche/droit.
> Touchez-vous le nez/la tête.
> Ouvrez la bouche.
> Fermez la bouche.
> Asseyez-vous!
> Levez-vous!
> (Think up some more for yourself . . .)

7
Quelle belle journée

(4 characters, 3 scenes)

E_____   Un estivant/Une estivante (A holidaymaker)
P_____   Un plagiste (A beach attendant)

Two young summer visitors   S_____ and L_____

Choose their names:

Les garçons	*Les filles*
Sebastian	Sabine
Serge	Séverine
Stéphane	Simone
Léon	Léonie
Lucien	Lise
Louis	Lola

*In Scene 1, S_____ and L_____, who are on holiday at the
seaside, decide to have a day on the beach. As the beach is
crowded, they put their things under a nearby beach umbrella
as they are going for a swim. The person who has rented the
umbrella (E_____) is annoyed to find the pile of clothes and
goes off to get the beach attendant (P_____).*

Scene 1

*(S_____ and L_____ are on their way to the beach. It is a
lovely day.)*

S: Quelle belle journée!

L: Je vais me baigner.

S: Moi, aussi!

(They arrive at the beach and see that it is very crowded)

L: Il y a du monde!

S: Il n'y a pas de place.

(L_____ spots a vacant beach umbrella)

L: Regarde ... Un parasol libre.

S: Formidable!

L: Laissons nos affaires ici.

*(They quickly get into their swimming things and put their
clothes and towels under the umbrella. As they move away, the
person who has hired the umbrella arrives and sees the pile of
things)*

E: A qui sont ces affaires? *(He looks angrily around for the
culprits)*

S: *(Seeing E_____'s annoyance, decides not to own up)* Je ne sais pas, monsieur/madame.

E: C'est mon parasol... à moi!

L: *(Guiltily)* Oh!...

E: Je vais chercher le plagiste... *(Goes off to find the attendant)*

S: *(To L_____)* Que faire?

L: *(Calmly)* C'est très simple. *(Picks up things and moves along the beach with them)*

In Scene 2, E_____ angrily explains the problem to the attendant (P_____), who comes over to the beach umbrella. As S_____ and L_____ have already moved their things, E_____ is very confused and apologises to P_____.

Scene 2

(E_____ finds the beach attendant and angrily complains)

E: Il y a des affaires sous mon parasol!

P: *(Anxious to please a customer)* C'est terrible, monsieur/madame.

E: Venez les voir!

P: Certainement, monsieur/madame.

E: Vous êtes le plagiste, n'est-ce pas?

P: Oui, monsieur/madame.

(They go over together to the beach umbrella and E_____ points angrily)

E: Voilà!

(*P_ _ _ _ _ views the now-empty space*)

P: Je ne vois rien, monsieur/madame.

E: (*Puzzled at the disappearance of the pile of things*) Comment? Je ne comprends pas!

P: (*Tactfully*) Cela ne fait rien.

E: Je m'excuse.

P: (*Moving away*) Au revoir, monsieur/madame.

(*E_ _ _ _ _ is left puzzling over what has happened*)

S_ _ _ _ _ and L_ _ _ _ _ have found a spot to eat their lunch but P_ _ _ _ _, overhearing their plans, warns them that picnicking is forbidden. They decide to swim but P_ _ _ _ _ indicates the red flag which means that this is not allowed. All that is left for them is sunbathing!

Scene 3

(*S_ _ _ _ _ and L_ _ _ _ _ have found a place on the beach to sit*)

S: (*Happily*) Et maintenant, le pique-nique!

L: Oh! J'ai faim!

(*P_ _ _ _ _, who is patrolling the beach, comes near and listens to their conversation*)

L: J'adore pique-niquer!

S: Du fromage!

L: Et du pain!

S: Et du vin!

L: Formidable!

 (P_____ moves up to them)

P: Pardon.

S: Oui?

L: Vous avez faim aussi?

P: Non.

S: Vous avez soif?

L: Prenez un verre!

P: Il est interdit de pique-niquer!

S: Comment?

L: Sur la plage?

P: Oui.

S: Oh, non . . .

L: *(Cheerfully accepting the situation)* Eh bien, allons nager.

P: Je regrette . . .

S: Je ne comprends pas?

P: Le drapeau rouge . . . *(Points to the red flag that is flying on a pole)*

L: Le drapeau rouge?

P: La mer est trop dangereuse.

S: *(Rather bitterly)* Nous pouvons prendre un bain de soleil?

P: *(With a smile)* Bien entendu!

 (S_____ and L_____ settle down to sunbathe and P_____ moves away)

In the alternative ending, a different disappointment lies in store for S_ _ _ _ _ and L_ _ _ _ _. Can you work out what it is and, perhaps, suggest some other 'disasters' that might stop the picnic?

Alternative ending

(S_ _ _ _ _ and L_ _ _ _ _ are sitting down on the beach and are about to start their picnic)

S: Où est le fromage?

L: Il est dans ton sac.

S: Non, il n'est pas là.

L: Où est le pain?

S: Il est dans ton sac.

L: Non, il n'est pas là.

S: Pas de fromage!

L: Et pas de pain . . .

S: Mais nous avons du vin?

L: Oui. As-tu le tire-bouchon?

S: Non, il est dans ton sac.

L: Je regrette, S_ _ _ _ _ . . .

S: J'ai une idée!

L: Oui?

S: Nous allons au restaurant!

L: Qui va payer?

S: Tu n'as pas d'argent?

L: *(Shakes his/her head)* Quelle belle journée!

(S_ _ _ _ _ and L_ _ _ _ _ gather up their belongings and go back home)

Et maintenant

Le Quiz

Tu es S_ _ _ _ _.

1 Quel temps fait-il?
Il fait_____.

2 Vas-tu te baigner?
Oui, je vais _____ baigner.

3 Y a-t-il de la place?
Non, il n'y a pas _____ place.

4 Où vas-tu laisser tes affaires?
Je vais les laisser _____ un parasol.

5 Est-ce ton parasol?
Non, ce n'est pas _____ parasol.

6 Que demandes-tu à L_ _ _ _ _?
Je lui _____, 'Que faire?'

7 As-tu faim?
_____, certainement.

8 Peux-tu pique-niquer?
Non, il est _____ de pique-niquer.

9 Peux-tu te baigner dans la mer?
Non, la _____ est trop dangereuse.

10 Peux-tu prendre un bain de soleil?
Oui, bien _____.

Et ensuite...

Le Jeu

Word ladders

There are lots of ways to make 'word ladders'.
Either a word is chosen and each letter becomes the
first letter of one of the 'rungs':

B e l l e
A u s s i
I n t e r d i t
G a g n e r
N o n
E s t i v a n t
R i e n

or using each of the letters of the chosen word as one of
the letters on each of the 'rungs'.

			f			
			r			
			o			
l		f	m	s	c	p
i	f	a	a	o	h	a
B	*A*	*I*	*G*	*N*	*E*	*R*
r	i	m	e	t	r	d
e	r				c	o
	e				h	n
					e	n
					r	e
						r

Work out one of each kind to give to an opponent,
but keep the vocabulary to one particular chapter.
    How many other ways can *you* make word
ladders?

8

Contrabande!

(4 characters, 3 scenes)

Two tourists   E_ _ _ _ _ and F_ _ _ _ _
Two Customs officers   N_ _ _ _ _ and O_ _ _ _ _

Choose their names:

Les garçons	*Les filles*
Édouard	Éliane
Éloi	Élise
Émile	Estelle
Fernand	Fabiola
Fabrice	Francine
Florian	Françoise
Norbert	Nadia
Noël	Nicole
Nestor	Nathalie
Omer	Odette
Oscar	Olga
Octave	Olivia

In Scene 1, two tourists are about to go through Customs. One is carrying a lot of things on which duty should be paid, but intends to go through the 'Nothing to Declare' exit. The other makes a bet that he/she will get caught!

Scene 1

(E_____ and F_____ have just got off the boat and are about to pass through Customs)

E: Avez-vous des cigarettes?

F: *(Calmly)* Oui, j'ai huit cents cigarettes.

E: *(Anxiously)* Où sont-elles?

F: Dans cette valise.

E: Avez-vous du vin?

F: Oui, neuf bouteilles.

E: *(More worried than ever)* Neuf bouteilles? Où sont-elles?

F: Dans ce sac, avec le whisky.

E: Du whisky? Alors, c'est tout?

F: *(Casually)* Non, j'ai trois montres.

E: *(Astonished)* Trois montres! . . .

F: Oui, une pour moi, et deux pour mes frères.

E: Où sont-elles?

F: Ici! *(Pulls up sleeve to reveal watches on wrist)*

E: Mais la douane?

F: Je n'ai pas peur de la douane.

E: Un douanier va vous arrêter.

F: Jamais!

E: Je vous parie vingt francs!

F: D'accord.
(They move together towards the green exit for 'Nothing to Declare')

In Scene 2, two Customs officers, N_ _ _ _ _ and O_ _ _ _ _, see the tourists talking. N_ _ _ _ _ thinks that E_ _ _ _ _ is behaving suspiciously.

O_ _ _ _ _ disagrees, but N_ _ _ _ _ makes a bet that E_ _ _ _ _ is a smuggler. N_ _ _ _ _ stops E_ _ _ _ _ but does not find any contraband.

Scene 2

(The two Customs officers are waiting at their desks to see the disembarking passengers. They see E_ _ _ _ _ and F_ _ _ _ _ in deep conversation.)

N: Regardez, O_ _ _ _ _!

O: Quoi?

N: Cette personne-là a un air suspect.

O: Vous croyez?

N: Regardez son visage . . .

O: Il/Elle parle à son ami/amie. C'est tout.

N: Il/Elle fait de la contrabande.

O: Vous êtes fou/folle.

N: Je vous parie vingt francs . . .

O: D'accord!

N: Moi, je vais l'arrêter ...

(N_ _ _ _ _ stops E_ _ _ _ _ as he/she goes through the green exit)

E: *(Nervously)* Bonjour.

N: Avez-vous des cigarettes?

E: Non, je ne fume pas.

N: Avez-vous du vin ou du whisky?

E: Non, je ne bois pas.

N: Avez-vous des cadeaux?

E: Oui, j'ai ce petit souvenir. *(Brings out cheap souvenir)*

N: C'est tout?

E: Oui.

N: Ouvre cette valise, s'il vous plaît.

E: Certainement.

(Opens case which N_ _ _ _ _ proceeds to search thoroughly, finding nothing)

N: *(Frustrated)* Bon ... vous pouvez passer!

(E_ _ _ _ _, very relieved, closes case, smiles nervously and leaves. F_ _ _ _ _, who has been watching, starts to follow.)

In Scene 3, O_ _ _ _ _ pleased to have won the bet, stops F_ _ _ _ _ who gives silly answers to the questions that O_ _ _ _ _ asks. O_ _ _ _ _ finds it all very amusing and lets F_ _ _ _ _ go through. Both F_ _ _ _ _ and O_ _ _ _ _ then claim their winning bets!

Scene 3

(O_ _ _ _ _ steps forward and motions F_ _ _ _ _ over to the desk)

O: Bonjour! *(Smiles)*

F: *(Cheerfully)* Bonjour.

O: Avez-vous des cigarettes?

(F_ _ _ _ _ has decided to give silly answers to try to seem innocent)

F: *(Jokingly)* Oh oui, j'ai ... trois mille cigarettes!

O: *(Joining in the joke)* Vraiment? Et du vin?

F: Oui, ... trente bouteilles de Beaujolais!

O: *(Laughing)* C'est vrai?

F: Et cinq litres de whisky!

O: Très amusant.

F: *(Confidentially)* J'ai aussi cent montres suisses ...

O: Vous êtes très drôle! ...

F: Vous ne m'arrêtez pas?

O: *(With a broad grin)* Mais non! ... Vous pouvez passer!

F: *(Laughing)* Merci! Au revoir.

(F_ _ _ _ _ joins E_ _ _ _ _ who has been waiting nervously. O_ _ _ _ _ goes over to N_ _ _ _ _)

F: *(To E_ _ _ _ _)* Mes vingt francs!

E: Ce n'est pas juste!

O: *(To N_ _ _ _ _)* Mes vingt francs!

N: Il n'y a pas de justice!

F_____ was very lucky: there are not many customs officers like that! See what happens this time as O_____ stops F_____.

Alternative ending (Starts from O_____ stopping F_____)

O: Bonjour. Avez-vous des cigarettes?

F: *(In a sincere way)* Oui, j'ai deux cents cigarettes.

O: *(In a friendly manner)* Avez-vous du vin?

F: Oui, quatre litres seulement.

O: C'est tout?

F: Oui.

O: Vous respectez le règlement?

F: Certainement.

O: Bon, vous pouvez passer.

F: *(Starting to move away from Customs)* Au revoir, et merci.

O: Oh! excusez-moi, monsieur/madame . . .

F: *(Turning)* Oui?

O: Quelle heure est-il, s'il vous plaît?

   (F_____ looks at his watch, thus uncovering the other watches)

F: Il est midi dix.

O: Ah! . . . quelles jolies montres!

F: *(Realises his mistake)* Oh, oui! . . .

O: Veuillez entrer dans mon bureau, monsieur/madame?

F: *(Worried)* Je peux expliquer . . .

O: Bien entendu!

   (F_____ and O_____ go into the office)

Et maintenant

Le Quiz

Tu es F_ _ _ _ _.

1 Combien de cigarettes as-tu?
   J'en ai _____ cents.

2 Où sont-elles?
   Elles sont dans ma _____.

3 As-tu du vin?
   Oui, j'en ai _____ bouteilles.

4 Combien de montres as-tu?
   J'en ai _____.

5 As-tu peur de la douane?
   Non, je n'_____ pas peur de la douane.

6 Combien pàries tu avec E_ _ _ _ _?
   Je _____ vingt francs avec E_ _ _ _ _.

7 Combien vas-tu gagner?
   Je vais gagner _____ francs.

8 As-tu de la contrebande?
   _____, j'ai de la contrebande.

9 O_ _ _ _ _, fouille-t-il/elle tes bagages?
   Non, O_ _ _ _ _ ne fouille pas _____ bagages.

10 Gagnes-tu les vingt francs?
   Oui, je _____ gagne!

Et ensuite . . .

Le Jeu

The Tray Game

Version 1

The teacher sets up a group of items on a tray,
or a desk, naming each one in French, giving
the spelling. You will then study them carefully
remembering each French name.

The teacher covers the items up so that they can
no longer be seen. A set time is then allowed for
you to write down a list of as many as you can
remember. (In French, of course!)

The teacher removes the cover and the lists are
checked.

Scoring: One point for each correct name.
(Minus one, for things *not* on the tray.)

Version 2

The teacher sets up and names the objects as
before. Then, out of sight of everyone, moves
the things around on the tray and takes one or
two of them away. You must spot the missing
items and write them down.

Scoring: One point for each object that you
spot is missing. Lose a point if you list it as
'missing' but it's still there.

9

Une Question de Chance

(3 or 4 characters, 3 scenes)

R_____ Un reporter sportif (A commentator)
C_____ Un caissier/Une caissière (A cashier)
(These two parts can be played by one person)

H_____ and L_____ Two friends at the races

Choose their names:

Les garçons	*Les filles*
Hector	Hélène
Honoré	Hilda
Hugues	Henriette
Igor	Inès
Ivan	Irma
Ignace	Isabelle

In Scene 1, H_____ and I_____ are going to the races. It is I_____'s first visit to a racecourse and H_____ is keen to give the impression of knowing a great deal about horses. H_____ tells I_____ that the horse I_____ has chosen has no chance of winning.

Scene 1

(H_____ and I_____ arrive at the racecourse and go to the turnstiles)

H: Deux entrées, s'il vous plaît.

C: Trente francs.

H: *(Hands over money)* Voilà. *(Takes tickets)* Et deux programmes, s'il vous plaît.

C: Six francs.

H: Voilà. *(Gives cashier money and takes programmes)* Merci.

C: Bonne chance!

(H_____ and I_____ go on to the paddock – le rond de présentation – and watch the horses being led round)

H: Voici les chevaux.

I: Quels beaux chevaux!

H: Le numéro deux, 'Pommier', est le plus beau.

I: Moi, je préfère le cheval numéro quatre, 'Robinetto'.

H: *(With the air of an experienced racegoer)* Il ne va pas gagner.

I: *(Surprised)* Pourquoi?

H: Il a un air fatigué.

I: *(Puzzled)* Vraiment?

H: Et il marche mal.

I: *(Anxiously)* C'est vrai?

H: Je n'aime pas son jockey.

I: *(Worried)* Pourquoi?

H: Il perd toujours.

> *(H_ _ _ _ _ nods knowingly. They move away from the paddock to the betting windows)*

In Scene 2, when H_ _ _ _ _ suggests they have a bet, I_ _ _ _ _ does not know how it is done. H_ _ _ _ _ explains where to put the money on and what to say but I_ _ _ _ _ decides to back 'Pommier', number four.

Scene 2

(H_ _ _ _ _ and I_ _ _ _ _ arrive at the betting windows – le pari mutuel)

H: Allons jouer!

I: Je ne comprends pas.

H: C'est très simple.

I: C'est vrai?

H: Oui. Vous dites 'Le deux . . . dix francs . . . gagnant.'

I: *(Puzzled)* Dix francs gagnant?

H: *(Enjoying the feeling of being 'the expert')* Où 'Le deux, dix francs . . . placé.'

I: *(Repeating carefully)* . . . dix francs placé . . .

H: Oui. Regardez là-bas. *(Pointing to the* pari-mutuel *windows)*

I: Les guichets?

H: Oui, les guichets à dix francs.

I: *(Goes to window)* Le quatre ... dix francs ... gagnant. *(Hands over money and takes ticket)*

H: *(Following at the window)* Le deux ... cent francs ... gagnant. *(Pays and takes ticket)*

I: Et maintenant?

H: Allons regarder la course!

(They go off to find a place in the grandstand)

*In Scene 3, H_ _ _ _ _ and I_ _ _ _ _ watch the race and listen to the commentator (*le reporter sportif*). There is great excitement and a photo-finish but I_ _ _ _ _'s horse is declared the winner. H_ _ _ _ _ is disappointed but puts I_ _ _ _ _'s success down to 'beginner's luck', and they go off to celebrate!*

Scene 3

(H_ _ _ _ _ and I_ _ _ _ _ are watching the race and listening to the commentary spoken over the loudspeakers by R_ _ _ _ _)

R: *(In a 'commentator's voice')* Les chevaux sont sous les ordres! *(The horses leave the starting stalls)* Partis!

I: *(Anxiously)* Je ne vois pas le quatre.

H: Le deux est en tête!

I: *(Disappointed)* Je vais perdre.

H: *(Excited)* Je vais gagner!

I: *(Desperately)* Allez le quatre! Plus vite . . .

H: *(Cheering)* Allez le deux . . .

R: *(Continuing the commentary)* Les chevaux entrent dans la ligne droite. C'est Pommier qui est en tête . . . suivi par Robinetto . . . *(Wtih rising excitement)* . . . Toujours Pommier . . . Puis Robinetto . . . Ils sont à égalité . . . Photo entre le deux et le quatre! *(R_____ is almost out of breath at the end of the commentary)*

H: C'est très serré.

I: *(Quite exhausted!)* Quelle course!

R: *(Slowly and clearly)* Le résultat de la première course:
Premier . . . le numéro quatre . . . Robinetto.
Deuxième . . . le numéro deux . . . Pommier.
Troisième . . . le numéro huit . . . Parasol.

I: *(Jumping about with excitement)* Bravo le quatre!

H: Oui. *(Half-heartedly)* Bravo . . .

I: Une boisson pour fêter mon succès!

H: Pourquoi pas! Aux innocents les mains pleines!

Alternative ending

There are many ways in which the race could have ended.
   1   H_____'s horse wins
   2   Both horses lose
   3   H_____'s horse wins but is disqualified
   4   I_____'s horse wins but is disqualified
   5   The race finishes in a dead heat
Imagine that you are the commentator. YOU can decide the result.

You prepare the race commentary and, when the race comes, you read out your commentary. Make sure that the others react to the 'new' result!

Voici des mots utiles:

le dead-heat – dead-heat
disqualifié – disqualified
une enquête – an inquiry

Et maintenant

Le Quiz

Tu es L_ _ _ _ _.

1. Combien coûtent les deux programmes?
   Les deux programmes coûtent _____ francs.

2. Quel cheval préfères-tu?
   Je préfère le cheval numéro _____.

3. Ton cheval, marche-t-il bien?
   Non, il marche _____.

4. Que dis-tu au guichet?
   Je dis, 'Le deux, dix francs _____.

5. Que fais-tu après?
   Je vais _____ la course.

6. Vois-tu le quatre?
   Non, je ne _____ vois pas.

7. Qui est en tête?
   C'est le _____ qui est en tête.

8. Vas-tu gagner?
   Non, je vais _____.

9. Quel est le résultat de la photo?
   C'est le _____ qui gagne.

10. Que vas-tu faire maintenant?
    Je vais acheter une _____ pour fêter mon succès.

Et ensuite . . .

Le Jeu

Le Grand Quiz

This is a game of skill and luck, like a very popular French radio quiz.

Contestants have two statements read out to them and must guess which one is true.

The first question is worth 2 points, the next is worth 4 points, then 8 points, and so on, up to a total of 512. However, it is not quite as simple as that!

If at any time you get an answer WRONG, you throw a dice to see if you can stay in the game.

If you throw a 1, 2 or 3 . . . you are eliminated and all the points you have won are cancelled.

If you throw a 6 . . . you are eliminated BUT keep HALF the points you have already won.

If you throw a 4 or a 5 . . . you get another chance at the same level. (If the answer to the new question is wrong, the dice-throwing starts all over again!)

WHEN YOU HAVE WON 32 POINTS, the dice must be thrown before each question to see if you can carry on.

If you throw a 6 . . . you leave the game but keep the points you have already won.

If you throw a 1, 2, 3, 4 or 5, you can carry on.

To start with, the statements from which a choice must be made by the contestant should be fairly simple, but after 32 points have been scored, they should become more difficult.

Questions can be read out either by the question-master, who is called *l'animateur* or *l'animatrice*, or anyone in the group. Questions should be written down in advance. The contestant is called *le concurrent* or *la concurrente*.

There will usually be a short 'chat' between the question-master (Q) and the contestant (C). For instance:

Q: Bonjour.

C: Bonjour.

Q: Quel âge avez-vous?

C: J'ai treize ans.

Q: Où habitez-vous?

C: J'habite à Londres.
etc.

Q: Bon. Pour deux points:
Affirmation A: Un tigre est un oiseau.
Affirmation B: Londres est en Angleterre.

C: Affirmation B.

Q: Réponse exacte! Maintenant, pour quatre points:
Affirmation A: Paris est la capitale de la Belgique.
Affirmation B: Le soleil est très chaud.

C: Affirmation A.

Q: Réponse fausse! Jetez le dé.
(C_____ throws the dice and gets a 4)

Q: Quatre! Bon. Pour quatre points . . .
etc.

The game can be played in two teams, with each team in turn being the contestant.

Statements (*Affirmations*) should be on DIFFERENT subjects. Do not give contradictory ones on the same subject as in:

A: Le soleil est chaud.

B: Le soleil est froid.

An example of a *harder* statement would be:

A: Un planeur est un outil.

B: Un orteil est un doigt de pied.

(B is correct. Un planeur [a glider] is not a tool, but un orteil [a toe] is another word for un doigt de pied!)

10

Les Pirates
négligents

(4 characters, 3 scenes)

4 Pirates

Barbe Bleue   (B_ _ _ _ _)
Barbe Grise   (G_ _ _ _ _)
Barbe Noire   (N_ _ _ _ _)
Barbe Rouge   (R_ _ _ _ _)

In Scene 1, the four pirates are getting bored with life at sea and decide to find a desert island where they can hide their treasure.

Scene 1

(The pirates are on the deck of the ship half-heartedly carrying out various tasks)

B: J'ai faim, moi.

G: J'ai soif, moi.

N: *(Yawns)* Je suis fatigué, moi.

(All three look at R_____, who is their leader)

R: *(Very positively)* Et moi, aussi!

B, G and N: *(Together)* Que faire?

R: Nous allons quitter le navire.

(B, G and N look at each other anxiously)

G: Avec le trésor?

R: *(Impatiently)* Bien sûr que oui!

N: *(Puzzled)* Où allons-nous?

R: A une île déserte.

B, G and N: *(Disbelievingly)* Quelle île déserte?

R: *(Pointing)* Regardez! Là-bas!

B, G and N: *(Together)* Une île déserte!

R: On y va ce soir...

B, G and N: *(Excitedly)* Oui, ce soir!

They go off to make preparations)

In Scene 2, the pirates go to the island at dead of night and bury the treasure.

Scene 2

(The pirates enter. B_____ and G_____ are carrying the treasure chest, which is very heavy. N_____ is carrying three spades. R_____ is in command.)

R: Mettez le trésor sous cet arbre.

B: Cet arbre-ci?

R: Oui. Faites un trou ici.

G: *(Puzzled)* Pourquoi?

R: Pour cacher le trésor!

(N_____ gives B_____ and G_____ a spade each and all three begin to dig. R_____ supervises operations.)

B: J'ai faim, moi.

G: J'ai soif, moi.

N: Je suis fatigué, moi.

R: *(Unmoved by their complaints)* Plus profond!

B: *(Fed up)* Zut alors!

G: *(Angry)* Sacrebleu!

N: *(Furious)* La barbe!

R: *(Ignoring their reactions)* Maintenant le coffre.

B: Il est lourd.

G: Nous sommes riches!

N: Je suis fatigué, moi.

R: Maintenant, bouchez le trou!

*(Without enthusiasm, the three start to fill up the hole.
R_____ supervises.)*

*The pirates decide to explore the island but find that it is a
dangerous place. There is no alternative but to return to their
ship. Alas, they forgot to make a plan of where they buried the
treasure...*

Scene 3

*(The burying of the treasure completed, the pirates are ready
to explore the island)*

R: Allons explorer!

B: *(Amazed)* Vous avez une carte?

R: *(Smugly)* Oui, un guide Michelin.

G: *(Disbelievingly)* De cette île déserte?

R: Naturellement.

N: *(With deep admiration)* Vous êtes très intelligent!

R: *(Modestly)* Merci.

B: Où sommes-nous?

R: *(Studying the map)* Nous sommes entre les sables
mouvants...

G: Oh!

R: Et le village des cannibales...

N: Oh!

R: . . . et la jungle . . .

B: Oh non!

R: . . . et les grottes de la mort.

B, G and N: *(Together)* Nous allons mourir!

B: *(Panicking)* Au navire!

G: *(Remembers the treasure)* Le trésor!

N: Vite!

B: Où est le plan?

R: *(Taken aback)* Quel plan?

G: Le plan du trou.

R: Je n'ai pas de plan.

B: Zut alors!

G: Sacrebleu!

N: La barbe!

R: Je crois qu'il est . . .

   *(B_____, G_____ and N_____ look accusingly at
   R_____)*

B: Creusez!

G: *(Hands R_____ a spade)* Voilà ma pelle!

N: Vite!

   (They watch as R_____ begins to dig)

*In the alternative ending they do have a map of where the
treasure is buried BUT three of them come to a sticky end!
Find out how, and then you can act it.*

B: Où est le plan?

R: Le voici. *(Reads)* 'Faites une ligne. Commencez au plus haut palmier.'

G: Ici.

N: Bon.

R: *(Reads)* 'Quinze pas à l'est . . .'

(They count aloud. A snake attacks B_____, who dies quietly.)

R: *(Reads)* 'Treize pas au nord . . .'

(They count aloud. G_____ falls into the quicksands and dies silently.)

R: *(Reads)* 'Quinze pas à l'ouest . . .'

(They count aloud. A spider kills N_____, who dies quietly.)

R: *(Reads)* 'Treize pas au sud . . .'

(He counts aloud) Et voilà! *(He turns round)* Comment?

(He cannot see the other pirates. He panics and runs towards the boat.)

R: Aïeeeeeee . . .!

Et maintenant

Le Quiz

Tu es Barbe Grise.

1 As-tu faim?
   Non, j'ai _____.

2 Où vas-tu?
   Je _____ à une île déserte.

3 Où mets-tu le trésor?
   Je mets le trésor _____ un arbre.

4 Fais-tu un trou?
   Oui, je _____ un trou.

5 Es-tu pauvre?
   Non, je _____ riche.

6 Connais-tu cette île déserte?
   Non, je _____ connais _____ cette île.

7 Barbe Rouge, a-t-il une carte?
   Oui, il _____ un Guide Michelin.

8 As-tu peur des cannibales?
   Oui, j'_____ peur des cannibales.

9 Où est le plan?
   Nous n'_____ pas de plan!

10 Donnes-tu ta pelle à Barbe Rouge?
   Oui, je lui donne _____ pelle.

Et ensuite . . .

Le Jeu

La Chasse au Trésor

Divide the group into two teams, and agree on a North/South line across the room. (The teacher's desk may make a good marker point for North.)

The aim of the game is to direct a member of the OPPOSING team, from the centre of the room to 'the treasure'. PIGEON STEPS (i.e. heel to toe, one foot after the other) will be used as PACES. The compass bearing will be given each time.

Only FIVE instructions are allowed. For example:

> Quatre pas au sud/six pas à l'ouest/huit pas au nord/deux pas à l'est/dix pas à l'ouest.

Organisation:

1 Everyone writes out their set of five instructions.
2 They then learn them by heart.
3 A 'treasure seeker' is chosen from the other team.
4 The written instructions are handed to the teacher.
5 The 'guide' gives the five instructions one by one, to the 'treasure seeker' who moves accordingly.

Scoring:

One point awarded for each correct instruction by the 'guide'.

One point awarded for each correct move by the 'seeker'.

NO points for an instruction that does not follow the written directions. NO points for a move either in the wrong direction OR with the wrong number of paces.

Vocabulary

a – from *avoir*: to have
à – to; at
   à l'heure – on time
adorer – to adore
les affaires – things
  aimable – nice, pleasant, likeable
  aimer – to like
un air – look; appearance
  aller – to go
  allons! – let's go!
  alors – then, so
un ami – a friend
une amie – a friend; a girlfriend
  amusant – funny; amusing
un an – a year
  anglais – English
un Anglais – an Englishman
une Anglaise – an Englishwoman
l'Angleterre – England
un apéritif – a pre-meal drink
  s'appeler – to be called
  appétit – see 'bon'
  apprendre – to learn
  appuie! – press! from *s'appuyer*:
  to press
une araignée – a spider
un arbre – a tree
  l'argent (m) – money
  arrêter – to stop (someone,
  something)
  arrêtez-vous! – stop!
  as–tu form of *avoir*
un ascenseur – a lift
  asseyez-vous! – sit down!
  attends! – wait!
  attention – see *faire*
  aussi – also, too

un autobus – a bus
  autre – other
  avec – with

les bagages – the luggage
se baigner – to go for a swim
un bain de soleil – see *prendre*
le ballon – the ball
la banque – the bank
une barbe – a beard
  la barbe! – blast!
  beacoup de – a lot of; lots of
  bien – well
    bien sûr – of course
    bien entendu – of course
  bientôt – soon
    à bientôt! – see you soon!
le billet – the ticket; banknote
une blague – a joke
  sans blague! – no kidding!
  Blanche-Neige – Snow White
la blanquette de veau – veal in a
  white sauce
  bleu – blue
  bois – from *boire*: to drink
la boisson – the drink
  bon (bonne f.*)* – good
    bon appétit! – enjoy your
    meal!
  bonjour – hello!, good morning!
  bonsoir – good evening!,
  goodnight!
la bouche – the mouth
  bouchez! – fill!
la bouteille – the bottle
le bouton – the button

le bruit – the noise
brun – brown
le bureau – the office

ça – that
    ça suffit! – that's enough!; that does it!
    ça va? – how are you?, how are things?
    ça va bien – very well, thanks
la cabine – the telephone kiosk
    cacher – to hide
le cadeau – the present, gift
le canard – the duck
le cannibale – the cannibal
le canot – the boat
la carafe – the decanter, carafe
la carte – the map; (restaurant) menu
ce – this, that
ces – these, those
c'est – it is, he is, she is
cela – that
    cela ne fait rien – it doesn't matter
cent – one hundred
    cinq cents – five hundred
certainement – certainly
la chasse – the hunt
le chauffeur – the driver
le chemin – the way
    cher – dear; expensive
    chercher – to look for
    chéri (chérie f.) – dear; darling
le cheval – the horse
la chèvre – the nanny goat
    choisi – chosen; from *choisir*: to choose
la chose – the thing
    chut! – ssh!
la classe – the class
    la salle de classe – the classroom
le coffre – the chest, safe
le coin – the corner

combien – how much?, how many?
comme – like, as
    et comme boisson? – and what would you like to drink?
commencer – to begin
comment? – how?, what?!
compliqué(e) – complicated, difficult
comprendre – to understand
compter – to count
conduire – to drive
    un permis de conduire – a driving licence
connaître – to know, to be acquainted with
continuer – to carry on
la contrebande – smuggling
    faire de la contrebande – to do some smuggling
le coq au vin – chicken cooked in red wine
courir – to run
    il court – he runs
    courant – running
    il entre en courant – he runs in
la crème – cream
    à la crème – in cream, with cream
creusez! – dig!
croire – to believe, think
    vous croyez? – you think so?
la cuisine – the kitchen
    quelle cuisine! – what good food!

la dame – the lady, woman
dans – in, into
de – of, from
d'accord – all right, OK
découvrir – to expose
déjeuner – to eat, to have a meal, to lunch
demander – to ask, to ask for
demi – half
derrière – behind

descendre de – to get out of
le désert – the desert
désirer – to desire; to want
désolé! – terribly sorry!
le dessert – the dessert, pudding
difficile – difficult
dix-huitième – eighteenth
le dommage – injury
c'est dommage! – what a shame!
donner – to give
la douane – the customs
le douanier – the customs officer
doucement – softly, quietly
droit – right
la droite – the right
à droite – on the right
tout droit – straight on
drôle – funny, amusing

une école – a school
écouter – to listen, to listen to
écrire – to write
l'égalité (f.) – equality
à égalité – neck and neck
en (prep.) – in
en retard – late
en (pronoun) – of it, of them
j'en ai deux – I have got two (of them)
je m'en vais – I'm off!
encore – again
un enfant – a child
entendu – see *bien*
entre – between
entrer (dans) – to go in, to enter
une erreur – a mistake
un escargot – a snail
l'essence (f.) – petrol
l'est – the east
un étage – a floor, storey
être – to be
excusez-moi! – excuse me!
je m'excuse – I'm sorry
expliquer – to explain

la faim – hunger
avoir faim – to be hungry
faire – to do, to make
que faire? – what are we going to do?
faites le plein – fill it up (car)
faites un trou – dig a hole
il fait beau – the weather is fine
faire attention à – to beware of
falloir – to be necessary
il faut – it is necessary
fatigué – tired
fermer – to shut, to close
fermé – closed, shut
le fermier – the farmer
fêter – to celebrate
la feuille – the sheet (of paper); the leaf
les feux (m.) – the traffic lights
la fois – the time, occasion
merci mille fois – many thanks
formidable! – super!, great!
fou (folle f.) – mad
fouiller – to search, to look through
le frère – the brother
le fromage – the cheese
fumer – to smoke

gagner – to win
dix francs gagnant – ten francs to win
la gare – the railway station
gauche – left
à gauche – on the left
le gendarme – the policeman
généreux – generous, kind-hearted
gentil – kind, pleasant
grand – big, tall
gris – grey
la grotte – the cave
le guichet – the ticket-office window
le guide – the guide book

habiter – to live in
haut – high, tall (not person)
  au plus haut – at the tallest
  tout haut – out loud
une heure – an hour
  à l'heure – on time
un homme – a man
  l'Homme Invisible – *The Invisible Man*

ici – here
une idée – an idea
il y a – there is, there are
une île – an island
innocent – innocent
  aux innocents les mains pleines!
  – beginners' luck
inquiet – worried, anxious

jamais! – never!
le jardin – the garden
le jeu – the game
jeune – young
joli – pretty, nice
jouer – to play; to place a bet (horseracing)
le jour – the day
la journée – the day
  quelle journée – what a day!
juste – fair
la justice – justice

là – there
  là-bas – over there
laisser – to leave
  laissez-moi tranquille! – leave me alone!
lever – to raise
  levez-vous! – stand up!
libre – free, unoccupied
la ligne – the line
  la ligne droite – the finishing straight
lire – to read
loin de – far from
lourd – heavy

magnifique – superb
la main – the hand
  le sac à main – the handbag
maintenant – now
mais – but
la maison – the house
mal – badly
manger – to eat
même – same, even
menaçant – threatening
merci – thank you
mettre – to put
meurt – from *mourir*: to die
midi – midday, noon
mille – a thousand
moi – me
  à moi – mine
le moment – the moment
  un moment! – hold on a moment!
mon (ma f., mes pl.) – my
le monde – the world
  il y a du monde! – there are a lot of people!
monsieur – mister, sir
monter – to go up
  monter dans une voiture – to get in a car
la montre – the wristwatch
mordre – to bite
la mort – death
le moteur – the engine
la moule – the mussel
mourir – to die
mouvant – moving
  les sables mouvants – quicksand

nager – to swim
le nain – the dwarf
  naturellement – naturally, of course
le navire – the ship
négligent – careless
la neige – the snow
noir – black

le nom – the name
   nom d'un chien! – blast it!
le nord – nord
   nous – we

un objet – an object
   occupé – occupied, busy
   ou – or
   où – where
l'ouest – west

le pain – the bread
le palmier – the palm tree
le panier – the basket
   paniquer – to panic
la panne – the breakdown
   en panne – broken down
le papier – paper
le parasol – the beach umbrella
   pardon! – excuse me!
   parier – to bet
   parler – to speak, talk
   pas – not
le pas – the step, pace
   passer – to pass, to overtake; to be on (at the cinema)
   pauvre – poor
   payer – to pay
la pelle – the spade
   perdre – to lose
    perdu – lost
le permis – the licence
   le permis de conduire – the driving licence
   petit – small
la peur – fear
   avoir peur – to be afraid
   peux – from *pouvoir*: to be able
la photo – the photograph
le pied – the foot
le piéton – the pedestrian
   pique-niquer – to picnic
la place – the place, room (space)
   placé – for a place
la plage – the beach

le plagiste – the beach attendant
   plaît – from *plaire*: to please
   s'il vous (te) plaît – please
le plan – the plan
   plein – full
   plus – more
   le plus – most
   ne ... plus – no longer
la poche – the pocket
le portefeuille – the wallet
   porter – to carry
le potage – the soup
   pour – for
   pourquoi? – why?
   pousser – to push
   pouvoir – to be able
   préférer – to prefer
   premier – first
   prendre – to take
   prendre un bain de soleil – to sunbathe
   presque – almost, nearly
   pressé – in a hurry
   prêt – ready
   prier – to beg, beseech
   je vous en prie – don't mention it
le problème – the problem
   prochain – next
   profond – deep
   puis – then

   quel (quelle f.) – what
   quel dommage! – what a shame!
   quinze – fifteen
   quitter – to leave
   quoi? – what?
   quoi, encore! – not again!

le raccourci – the short cut
   ramasser – to pick up
   rapidement – quickly
   rassurez-vous – don't worry
la reconnaissance – the recognition
   reconnaître – to recognise
   regarder – to look at, to watch

le règlement – the regulations
rencontrer – to meet
le rendez-vous – the meeting
rentrer – to return
respecter – to abide by, comply
with
le retard – lateness
  en retard – late
se retourner – to turn round
  revoir – to see again
  au revoir – goodbye
le rez-de-chaussée – the ground
floor
  riche – rich
  rien – nothing
    cela ne fait rien – it doesn't
    matter
  rire – to laugh
    en riant – with a laugh
  rouge – red
  rouler – to drive
la route – the route, the way
la rue – the street

le sable – the sand
  les sables mouvants – the
  quicksand
le sac – the bag
  le sac à main – the handbag
  sacrebleu! – blast!
la salade – the salad
le sang – the blood
  bon sang! – blast!, goodness!
  sans – without
  savoir – to know (a fact)
la semaine – the week
le serpent – the snake
  seulement – only
  si – if; so
la soif – thirst
  avoir soif – to be thirsty
le soir – the evening
  sortir – to go out
    sors-tu? – are you going out?
le succès – the success
le sud – south

suffire – to be enough
  ça suffit – that's enough!
la Suisse – Switzerland
  sûr – sure, certain
    bien sûr – of course
  sur – on
  suspect – suspicious

se taire – to be quiet
  tais-toi! – be quiet!
le tarif – the price list
le taureau – the bull
  téléphoner – to telephone
la tête – the head
  en tête – in the lead
la tire – see *vol*
le tire-bouchon – the corkscrew
  tirer – to shoot
  toi – you
  tomber – to fall
le ton – the tone
  d'un ton menaçant – in a
  threatening tone of voice
  touchez-vous! – touch!
  toujours – always
  tout – all
    toute la population – the whole
    population
    à tout à l'heure! – see you
    later!
  treize! – thirteen
  trente – thirty
  très – very
le trésor – the treasure
  la chasse au trésor – the
  treasure hunt
  triomphant – triumphant
  trop – too
le trou – the hole
  trouver – to find
la tulipe – the tulip

  vais, vas, va – from *aller*: to go
la valise – the suitcase
  venir – to come
  veuillez – kindly

veux – from *vouloir*: to want
vient – from *venir*: to come
la ville – the town
le vin – the wine
vingt – twenty
vingtième – twentieth
vite – quickly
voici – here is, here are
la voie – the track (railway)
voilà – there is, there are
    les voilà! – there they are!
voir – to see
la voiture – the car; the carriage
le vol – the theft
    le vol à la tire – pickpocketing

le voleur – the thief
    le voleur à la tire – the pickpocket
vouloir – to want
le voyage – the journey
vrai – true
    c'est vrai? – is that so?
vraiment – really

les yeux (m.) – the eyes
    (un oeil – an eye)

zut! – blast!